DISMANTLED DAMSEL

Copyright © 2025 by Kiante' Phelps-Woods

All rights reserved. No part of this book may be reproduced or used in any manner without the written permission of the copyright owner except for the use of quotations in a book review.

979-8-9926704-0-0
Imprint: Kamp Woods
For more information, address:
KAMPWOODSINFO@GMAIL.COM

Second Edition

Dedication

This book has always been a conversation with self, spirit, and sisterhood. But it wouldn't exist without the community who has held me through the becoming.

The second edition of Dismantled Damsel is dedicated to my friends, family, and mentors who have provided insight and guidance throughout my life, aiding me in becoming the woman I am growing into today.

I want to begin by thanking all the artists and creatives who share their expressions with the world. Their contributions have allowed me to witness beauty and have inspired me to add my creativity to the canvas of our collective community.

I would also like to thank Vickie Jackson for endlessly pouring into me with wisdom, encouragement, and guidance that continues to benefit me throughout my life. Her belief in my greatness and her prayers for my spirit's protection are rooted in the foundation of my legacy. Because of her, I am who I am, and for that, I will always be thankful.

Next, I want to thank my beautiful sisters—Desiree, Sequeria, Kennedy, Kayla, Kaycee, and Hailey—for always being a source of light, love, and validation in the life experiences we share. I will forever cherish the memories we've made and the bond we share.

Because of them, I am who I am, and for that, I will always be thankful.

I also want to thank Ms. Tanya for her honesty, kindness, and selflessness in sharing her strengths. Her love and friendship are treasured gifts that have significantly impacted my journey into adulthood.

Because of her, I am who I am, and for that, I will always be thankful.

I deeply appreciate the lessons and gifts I've received from everyone who has chosen to support me. Lastly, I want to thank the next generation of young ladies, including Aaryah and Jolin, for reminding me to stay in touch with my dreams and to always be fearless in pursuing them.

FOREWORD

Dismantled Damsel was never meant to be a one-time expression. From the beginning, it was envisioned as a living, breathing testament to transformation—a mirror held up to the raw, radiant complexity of womanhood. As this second edition enters the world, I am reminded that growth is never linear, and healing doesn't come in one draft.

This edition is rooted in gratitude. It would not exist without the tribe of individuals who have poured into me with love, insight, and truth. To my friends, family, and mentors—you are the backbone of my becoming. Your guidance continues to mold me into the woman I am proud to evolve into, day by day.

Dismantled Damsel remains what it always was—a movement. A permission slip to come undone. A spark to ignite healing. A soft but steady light in a dark room. This second edition carries deeper reflections, more intentional gratitude, and a wider embrace of all that we are and are becoming.

This book is a witness to all who've loved me into myself. It is our reflection, our unraveling, our rebuilding. And it still stands as a testament to the duality and depth of feminine expression—a space where we come undone not to fall apart, but to be made new.

This is the second chapter in a story that continues to rise. This is Dismantled Damsel—rebirthed, reimagined, and rooted deeper than before.

—Kamp Woods

AWAKEN

THIS IS AN ODE ADDRESSED TO
WOMEN & DAUGHTERS,
WHO FOUND THEMSELVES
DISMANTLED BY FRACTURED
RELATIONSHIPS WITH LOVERS &
FATHERS.
WHO UNWILLINGLY SACRIFICE
THEIR SANITY TO BECOME
MOTHERS & MARTYRS.
THIS IS TO THE MANY BLACK
WOMEN
WHO ARE SUFFERING &
DEPRESSED.
TO THE MASS OF DARK DAMSELS
DYING IN DISTRESS.
THIS IS FOR THE STARTLED &
SOFT-SPOKEN,
FOR THOSE READY TO AWAKEN
FROM SELF-INFLICTING TORTURE,
THERE IS ALWAYS MORE LIFE TO
LIVE & IN THE END,
MOST WILL APPRECIATE THAT
THEY DID.

RUMINATION

WOMANHOOD IS MOST
FRAGILE WHEN IT'S ONLY
BEGUN. MOST ANGELS GET
THEIR WINGS & STILL FLY
TOO CLOSE TO THE SUN.
PREPARED WITH THE SECRET
OF THE BEES,
MOST WOMEN STILL GET
STUNG.
&
HOW CAN ONE ESCAPE
THEMSELVES,
WHEN THERE IS NOWHERE TO
RUN?

CRISIS CRY

Our lambs were never silent.
They've shared pleas for help through the slaughter & the violence.
Some have protested, while others choose to riot,
regardless they can collectively agree that they're tired of dying.
The ghetto cries to God in gospel,
with questions of how this treacherous reality is still possible?
Will black people ever be free or forever remain held hostage?

DEPENDENCE

Mom and Dad are out of sight,
So, we had permission to go out of our minds.
My lungs were filled with confetti,
&
I held my breath long enough to have a
permanent taste of the party.
We weaved and rolled to the beat of the same brief ballad.
While trading kisses and touches of our tongue pallets.
Like Alice with the rabbit, we were friends for every second of convenience.
Sharing half-truths glued together as a reason,
To justify our behavior and acting out as heathens.

STUBLE SIGNS

IF MY WALLS COULD SPEAK,
THEY'D DISCUSS MY TEAR STAIN
SHEETS
&
MY CONSTANT ACCEPTANCE OF
DEFEAT.
THEY'D TELL THE TRUTH OF
HOW MY MOODS CAN SWING FASTER
THAN THE SPEED OF LIGHT &
MY BATTLES WITH THE DARKNESS
THAT HAUNTS THE NIGHT. THEY'D
TELL YOU TO COUNT THE BOTTLES
UNDER MY BED
&
MENTION THE CONVERSATIONS
WITH VOICES IN MY HEAD.
IF MY WALLS COULD SPEAK,
WOULD YOU LISTEN OR IGNORE
THEM INSTEAD?

TIMEBOMB

MY BACK IS AGAINST A WALL
THAT'S SCHEDULED FOR DEMOLITION.
WHAT'S YOUR MISSION WHEN YOU'RE INVADING MY VISIONS?
I THOUGHT THE GLASS WAS HALF FULL BUT YOU ASSURED ME THAT IT IS EMPTY.
YOU FILL THE CIRCLES UNDER MY EYES
BUT I CAN'T TELL IF MORE OF THE BRUISES COME FROM YOUR HANDS OR MINE.
WITH NO EXIT SIGN & NO WARNING,
HOW DO I ESCAPE WHEN I'M FREEFALLING?

UNDER PRESSURE

I can not say I am stable,
when in reality,
my sanity is a fable.
I'm scared of my reflection &
have spent too many years
accepting abuse and neglection.
How loud must I cry before
I get close to an answer to why?
Can any of you see,
that perhaps I am
not prepared for
what life has in
store for me?

RUMINATION PT.2

If I can stand, then why am I falling?
Is it yours or my eyes that can't stop crying? Tell me, why should I hold on if you are comfortable dying?
Does it make sense to stay when I'm the only one trying?
Tell me, when did you cage your lion?
When did you start lying?
As you sink further into the dark, did you discover anything worth finding?
Tell me, was it worth it to go out in the rain only to get struck by lightning?
When did the thought of death become so exciting?

INHERENCE

Last night she flew,
but I wonder if she knew,
that night I stumbled behind her in the same shoes.
We are a mother & daughter drunken by fermented fruits,
and emotionally exhausted by swinging moods.

SOLITUDE

I slid into Frank's Ocean & almost drown. Like a tree all alone when I fell,
I didn't make a sound.
For when I am lost,
I'd rather not be found.

HARD CANDY

Reality bit my lip & brought blood to the skin. No longer can I walk through life, believing consequences are pretend.
The plan was always fuck jobs, but never to reside under a bridge.
However, I've learned that sometimes, standing on the edge can give you reasons to live.

BEST FOOT FORWARD

Sometimes, my glowing
sun descends
on the gray clouds.
I'm weighed down by the
heavy rain
that didn't fall that
day.
I'm surrounded &
suffocated by the mist
around me.
I'm touched & tortured
by things I don't want
to feel.
Not long enough for
them to take over, but
just enough for me to
wonder if it is real.
My sun will rise again,
hopefully, tomorrow
will be a clear sky

GENERATIONAL CURSE

This time last year,
I tried to dance to dodge bullets
but fatally got tattooed by pistols.
I met my best buds in an ashtray,
&
allow them to paint my lips crimson with nightly kisses…
My only crime is intoxication
&
as a result, I'm often tortured by a tangled tongue.
I can't help myself from choking on love languages that I speak with slurs.
The shame ignites me,
Somehow, it excites me.
I've learned to keep my eyes wide till the sun rotates with no expectations for what awaits... Will this year serve as blank memory or aimlessly mimic another mistake?

ENLIGHTEMENT

It all started in
April & ended in May.
I used my bike to
take a trip,
that lasted four
days.
Through it all,
truths were exposed &
I began to pray.
I said,
Dear God,
I called on you today
to offer thanks for
showing me the way.
For without your
guidance, I'd surely
be lost in this maze.
And for that, you
live in my heart,
where all love stays.

UNSPOKEN DESIRE

Please blow me a kiss filled with the taste of yellow in a balloon-filled backyard.
I want to sway to the heartbeat of newly born happiness
&
focus only on the direction our dreams are headed in.
I want us to capture flaming paper planes piloted by driven depression determined to ruin our sunrise.
I want to be defined only by
pleasure & to have the reality we exist in mirror our desires come true.

INTIMATE EXCHANGE

The sweat of summer stuck to our skin
&
Roaming around after dark led to only one deed being done.
The forces of nature worked together for the night.
Allowing the stars to enlightened us to the possibility of lust.
The moonlight guided us to the promised land Starting with ...
You
Touching me
Exploring your mental visions in real-time
You pinched me
&
Who knew damp dreams could come true?
I
Finally, have my fingers entangled in your fibers. My palms found sensation gliding along
each exposed piece of you.
Who knew clothes hid so much?

US
HOLDING TIGHT,
ONLY LETTING GO OF
EVERYTHING WE'VE HELD BACK.
I
MOANED OUT LOUD THE
TREASURE MAP, LEADING **Y**OU
TO ENTER JUST WHERE **X**
MARKED MY SPOT

TRAINED HELPLESSNESS

HE DROVE ME CRAZY,
WITH A TIGHT GRIP
ON THE STEERING
WHEEL.
HE TOOK POSSESSION
OF MY PETALS,
&
FONDLED MY FLOWERS
AT HIS LEISURE.
ONLY TO LEAVE ME
POLLINATED WITH
POISON,

I MISTOOK AS
CONFIRMATION OF
BEING CHOSEN.

SENSUAL CONFESSION

SEX IS LIKE A DESPERATE DESIRE FOR OUR BODIES TO CONVERSE.
THE ONLY WAY TO SATISFY ME FROM DYING THIRST. A CHANCE FOR US TO EXCHANGE A DIALOGUE THAT'S UNIQUELY REHEARSED.
AS OUR TONGUES EXPLORE & LICK,
CANDLES BURN DOWN TO THEIR WICKS.
YOU RUB & TEASE,
TICKLE THE LIPS ABOVE MY KNEES.
ALLOWING ME TO BLESS YOU WITH BLOSSOM & SHARE A SENSUAL SQUEEZE

WHITE LIGHTER

You're as pleasant as a
jacket covered puddle,
absorbed with dank
misfortune.
Your nose bled through the
pages of
this week's fable.
You tell me it all started
with
Trying to learn a language
Just by inhaling it.
I'm in love with the
absence of leisure
&
have felt the prick of
plastic kisses more than
enough
I took you as someone who
Functions through static...
Not one who would
Eventually, shock me

THOUGHT SCARIER THAN THE DARK

WAS IT THE MONSTERS
UNDER MY BED, OR I
WHO HAUNTS THE
NIGHT INSTEAD?

EXPOSURE

I TRAVELED TO A DIFFERENT DIMENSION, WITH HOPES TO DISCOVER FACT IN FICTION.
IN THE DEPTHS OF DEMISE, I WITNESSED WITH MY EYES, DEMONS DISGUISED AS DAMSELS.
I SPOKE TO THE HOSTAGES HELD IN THEIR HALLOW HEARTS & FOUND THEM DECAYING FROM IMPOVERISHED INDIGNITY.
I'M DISAPPOINTED BUT NOT SURPRISED, TO FIND TRUTH HIDDEN IN THEIR LIES.

HEARTBREAK

When you said you needed space, I sent smoke signals to Saturn in hopes that you'd be able to recognize and break old patterns. However, you stated: one cannot control what is created or destroyed & the same goes for our matters.

CONSEQUENCES

She's branded by a culture that surfs crowds and couches.
A loose lover that can't help but swing on a carousel of collision
The ocean slides from her eyes & she rides constant waves of commotion.
Instead of love, unfamiliar limps and loins maneuver through her collapsed castle
Blame escapes emotion in exchange for blistering ulcers of shame

ROCK BOTTOM

MY PIECE OF MIND BECAME BURIED UNDER THE SKELETONS IN MY CLOSET

&

COULD ONLY BE FOUND AFTER I THOUGHT I COMPLETELY LOST IT.

ABANDOMENT

I HAVE A MORNING
JACKET,
BUT I SHIVER IN
THE EVENING. FOR
I'D RATHER BE
ALONE,
THAN ACCOUNTABLE
FOR LEAVING.

LEARNED BEHAVIOR

I USED TO FOLLOW MY FRIEND,
TO WHERE THE SIDEWALK ENDS.
I SAW SOME THAT WERE SNEAKING OUT,
WHILE OTHERS WERE BEING FORCED IN.
SKIN TO SKIN,
LIMB TO LIMB,
AFTER THOSE NIGHTS,
WE'D NEVER BE THE SAME AGAIN.
WE CRAWLED THE STREETS
&
FOUND STRANGERS IN SHEETS,
ONLY TO TRADE SINS IN EXCHANGE FOR SOMEWHERE TO SLEEP. I USED TO FOLLOW MY FRIEND,
TO THE PEEL IN THE PAVEMENT.
A PLACE THAT ALLOWED ME TO KEEP MY MIND VACANT.
WE WERE VIRGINS TO CLARITY
&
IN A DESPERATE SEARCH FOR STIMULATION, SIMILARITY, OR SANITY.

WE FOUND LOVE IN IMPROPER
EXPRESSIONS,
THE KIND THAT IS ONLY GIVEN
WHEN WE WERE UNDRESSING.
I LOVE HER & LIFE
BUT TO KNOW BETTER NOW IS
TRULY A BLESSING.
I EXCHANGED CHILDHOOD
INNOCENCE FOR THE LIFE OF A
MILD-DEGENERATE.
I FOUND MYSELF RUNNING,
UNTIL I WAS CAUGHT
& I WAS FORCED TO UNLEARN
EVERYTHING I WAS
TAUGHT.

WITHDRAWAL SYMPTOMS

MY HANDS SHAKE,
BUT I KNOW I'M NOT NERVOUS.
MY CRIES FOR HELP ARE SO LOUD,
I KNOW DEATH CAN HEAR ME FLIRTING.
I STUCK & POKE MY OWN DOTS
TILL BLOOD REACHES THE SURFACE,
AND I FIND MYSELF WONDERING IF
IF I COME DOWN FROM THE HIGH WERE THE WINGS EVER WORTH IT?

Beneath the Baddest

She's Lisa Bright &
Dark.
Similar to Mona,
a mastered work of art.
She's a dark fantasy,
a wicked woman
naturally.
She's addictive like
nicotine,
a sweet taste that
leaves a sting.
But ultimately she's
just a caged bird,
who never learned to
fly on broken wings.

REBORN

I WAS CALLED TO THE BLIND SPOT IN THE BACK OF MY MIND.
A PLACE OF MADNESS IN MOTION, DELAYED DIALECT, AND TERRIBLE MISUSE.
A PLACE SO UNTAMED WITH A NUMBER OF SCREWS LOOSE.
I'VE DRIFTED AS FAR AS NEPTUNE AND ONLY AFTER BEING SAVED, I CAN NOW SHARE THE TRUTH.
THAT ONE CAN'T EXPECT THE BODY TO BE NOURISHED, WITHOUT THE INTAKE OF SPIRITUAL FOOD.
AND ONLY WITH SUBMISSION TO THE FLESH OF YOUR FEELING, CAN ONE TRULY COMMENCE THEIR JOURNEY OF HEALING.

FLIPPED SCRIPT

WITH THE ABSENCE OF
BEING RAISED,
ONE MUST RISE, RID
THYSELF OF CONGESTED
TESTIMONY LODGED BETWEEN
CRIES FOR HELP &
SETTLEMENT. FORGET THE
GRIEF OF LOST TIME,
&
HOLD ON TO THE HANDS OF
SOMETHING
THAT GOES FURTHER THAN
JUST AROUND.
THIS MESSAGE ISN'T LACED
SO NO CHANCE FOR A GUILT
TRIP.
PLEASE,
LOVE YOURSELF.

Love Letter

Kiss me with a wide open mouth,
& don't forget to party till the freckles fall off.
I want to laugh so loud we forget our doubts & disappear into ourselves that people question our whereabouts.
I love you like my favorite color
& regarding you,
I'd never trade for another.

MENTAL MASTERY

With no help from the white rabbit,
I fell deep into a hole of bad habits.
Even before 21, I was a savage & had done enough damage to the point of no salvage.
Although life can appear to be lavish,
I learned quickly that internal demons are always ready to ravish.
Be careful who you pray to and what you call magic.
Because what starts off sweet, often turns tragic.

LOVERS TURNED ENEMIES

I'LL NEVER FORGET THE
FORMULA OF YOUR
CHEMISTRY,
AND HOW IT FELT TO MATCH
YOUR ENERGY.
WHAT WAS PROMISED TO BE
FOR INFINITY,
IS NOW JUST A SWEET
MEMORY.

CLOUDED QUESTIONS

WHAT'S THE DIFFERENCE BETWEEN AN EXORCISM AND BIRTH?

HOW DO YOU KNOW IF YOU WERE POISONED BY THE BREAST THAT WAS USED TO NURSE?

WHAT DOES THE MIND LOOK LIKE WHEN IT'S ON THE BRINK OF BURST?

&

EVEN WITH SOLITUDE, WILL **I** EVER COME FIRST?

RUMINATION, INTERRUPTED

The party started next door and didn't stop till the bodies hit the floor.
I found my center, but it was rotten from the core.
However, just like the ocean, there's more to explore.
And how can one be caged if a change in mentality unlocks the door?

PURPOSE

IS DEATH THE ONLY
PASSAGE TO HEAVEN?

OR CAN IT BE FOUND ON
EARTH BY BECOMING A
LIVING LEGEND?

ATTENTION DEMAND

EVERYTHING CREATED CAN ALSO BE DESTROYED. BE CAREFUL WITH THE DISTRACTIONS YOU USE TO FILL YOUR VOID.

WOMAN TO WOMAN

TO THE LADY WHO SING MY BLUES,
WITH BALLADS AND LYRICS THAT GUIDE ME WITH THE WITS IN WHAT TO DO.
I ASK YOU TO BLESS ME WITH THE PROTECTION TO RELEASE WHAT I MUST LOSE & AVOID THOSE THAT MISHANDLE AND ABUSE.
GRANT ME THE STRENGTH TO NAVIGATE THIS LIFE THAT OFTEN LEAVES SO MANY CONFUSED.

MIRROR REFLECTION

The voices echo & vibrate,
similar to the motions of an earthquake.
I'm mesmerized by landscapes but held prisoner by the chatter of my mind I can't escape.

Thoughts and impulses, so much to contemplate.
Running sounds ideal, but I've learned one can't fix what is not faced.

TRANSYLVANIA

THERE'S CAVITIES IN MY CRANIUM,
DISGUISED AS DISSOCIATION AND MANIA.

MANIC MONDAY

The girls who are interrupted live in a reality full of glitches.
My **e**motional wounds can't be repaired with snitches.
Even with the feelings buried in the deepest of ditches.
So I ask nicely,
Can you be my witness and capture my kaleidoscope of kisses?

BIRTHDAY WISHES

If you're reading this
It's too late,
I already made a fatal mistake.
By blowing out the candles before receiving the cake.
With too much at stake
How could one not crumble under the weight?

FEELING THOUGHTS

WE NEVER KNOW
HOW MUCH WE MISS
BEING
DISTRACTED...
IN ATTEMPTS TO
NUMB OURSELVES
AND CONTINUE TO
HACK IT. ..
THE PRESSURE IS
TIGHTER THAN A
PACKET...
WITH LIMITED
HEALTHY
TACTICS...

MANIC MONDAY

You can't be scared of my darkness but also stay in my light. Remember to conquer your fears and embrace your might. And don't be afraid to mix colors & make something new of the black & white.

SUPPRESSED EXPRESSION

GIOVANNI'S ROOM IS HOT AND STICKY.
I ONLY PULLED YOU IN CLOSE TO CONFIRM THAT YOU MISSED ME.
IF YOU DESIRE MORE, I'LL GIVE YOU PLENTY.
IT'S NOW OR NEVER, MOVE INTENTLY.

ANSWERED PRAY

MY FATHER TOOK
ME WITH
STRETCHED HANDS
AND
REMINDED ME
THAT I'M A PART
OF GODS PLAN.

GENTLE COMFORT

Celebrate life from conception to death.
For one never knows which inhale will be their last breath.

INFLATED EGO

ARE YOU THE SMARTEST IN THE ROOM **O**R JUST THE LOUDEST? HOW CAN YOU PROVIDE GUIDANCE WHEN YOUR JUDGEMENT IS CLOUDED? WHY WOULD **I** FOLLOW YOUR DREAMS IF YOU VISIBLY DOUBT IT?

About the Author

Kamp Woods, a vibrant and emerging voice in the literary world, hails from the culturally rich landscapes of Houston, Texas. As a young African American woman, Kamp is deeply influenced by the tapestry of creativity woven within her family and the dynamic artistic community surrounding her.

Debuting onto the literary scene with her mesmerizing poetry collection, "Dismantled Damsel," Kamp Woods takes readers on an evocative journey through the intricate realms of femininity, spirituality, and personal growth. Her words are not just verses on a page but a testament to the resilience of the human spirit and a celebration of the multifaceted nature of womanhood. Her debut collection is only the beginning of what promises to be a remarkable journey, inviting readers to join her in exploring the boundless realms of creativity and self-discovery.

Beyond the written word, Kamp Woods is a multifaceted creative force with upcoming projects that promise to captivate audiences across different artistic mediums. Whether through poetry, visual arts, or other creative endeavors, she continues to carve a unique space for herself in the world of art and expression.

www.ingramcontent.com/pod-product-compliance
Lightning Source LLC
Chambersburg PA
CBHW042340150426
43195CB00006B/116